NATIONAL GEOGRAPHIC
School Publishi

It's Electrifying

PATHFINDER EDITION

By Sara Cohen Christopherson

CONTENTS

It's Electrifying

Somewhere, at this very moment, lightning is striking our planet. Every minute nearly 1,800 thunderstorms are brewing somewhere in Earth's sky.

Those storms can create about 40 lightning strikes each second. Many storms make even more. Some large storms can generate 425 lightning flashes a minute. During one storm in 1953, more than 600 flashes a minute lit the sky.

Lightning is actually a supercharged bolt of electricity. **Electricity** is a form of energy in which tiny particles called electrons move. A single bolt of lightning can contain billions of watts of electrical power.

Have you ever been shocked when you touched a doorknob? If you have, you might even have seen a spark. That type of electricity, called static electricity, is similar to what causes lightning. Positive and negative charges attract and—ZAP!—lightning strikes.

Where does this electricity come from? This electricity builds up inside clouds. Clouds are made of dust and water droplets. Wind blows the dust and droplets around inside the cloud. This makes a positive charge at the top of the cloud. It also makes a negative charge at the bottom.

The ground below a thundercloud has a positive charge. Lightning flashes between areas with opposite charges.

1. The top of a cloud has a positive electrical charge.

2. The bottom of a cloud has a negative electrical charge.

3. The ground below a thundercloud has a positive charge.

4. When the positive and negative electrical charges get strong enough, lightning flashes between the cloud and the ground.

5. Lightning also flashes between the top and bottom of a cloud.

Kinds of Lightning

Lightning comes in many different forms. Here are a few kinds you might see in your neighborhood.

Forked lightning looks like tree branches.

Sheet lightning is a flash of lightning inside a cloud.

Heat lightning is a flash of lightning that is so far away you cannot hear the thunder it makes.

A Big Bolt

If you were close up to lightning, what would you see? An actual bolt is only 1–2 inches wide. Although lightning is narrow, it can be very long. The longest lightning bolt recorded was 189.9 kilometers (118 miles)!

Lightning is hot enough to melt metal. It is also hot enough to melt sand and rock. In fact, lightning is even hotter than the sun!

City Lights. Lightning strikes the Empire State Building in New York City. A lightning rod at the top keeps the building safe.

Lightning Strikes!

Some parts of Earth have more lightning than others. In the United States, lightning strikes most frequently in Florida, in the area between Tampa and Orlando. Almost all of the lightning strikes there happen between May and October. This is because of moisture and temperature conditions that lead to storms.

Spark of Inspiration. Benjamin Franklin flew a kite during a thunderstorm in 1752. That helped him prove that lightning is made of electricity.

Sparking Safety

Lightning can be destructive. It starts fires, causes power outages, and damages buildings. All that destruction adds up. Lightning causes hundreds of millions of dollars of damage yearly. Lightning can also be dangerous. Each year in the United States lightning kills about 70 people and injures 300 others.

For years, scientists have been trying to protect people from lightning. In the 1750s, Benjamin Franklin came up with the idea of a lightning rod. A lightning rod is a piece of metal that is placed on the top of a building. The metal is connected to the ground by a long wire. When lightning strikes the rod, the wire carries the electricity safely to the ground. The building does not get damaged.

It is important to go inside at the first sign of a thunderstorm. If there are no buildings nearby, being inside an automobile is safer than being outside in the storm.

Watch Out!

- **Check the weather.** Before you go outside to exercise or play, find out what the weather will be like. Stay home if a bad storm is on its way.
- **Don't fool around.** Lightning is powerful stuff. Don't wait until a storm is on top of you. Go inside at the first sign of thunder or lightning.
- **Find shelter.** Porches and open shelters aren't safe during a storm. Go inside a building. If there are no buildings, a car will also do.
- **Stay away from trees.** Standing under a tree might help you stay dry—but it's the last place you want to be in a lightning storm.

What Makes Thunder Rumble?

Flash! You see a bolt of lightning. Boom! You hear thunder. Why does thunder follow lightning?

Lightning is super hot. A bolt heats the air to more than 23,871°C (43,000°F). Air is made of tiny parts called molecules. Lightning makes these tiny parts of air move quickly apart.

After lightning strikes, the air cools. The tiny parts of air move closer together again. The air moves so fast that it makes a sound. We call that sound thunder.

An Electrifying Idea

The electricity in a single lightning bolt is enough energy to power a 100-watt lightbulb for three months. So why don't we use lightning to produce electrical energy?

The idea of capturing the electricity in lightning has been around for a long time. But no one has come up with a system that works. Still, some inventors keep trying. Maybe it will happen in the future.

The next time you see a lightning flash, think about what type of lightning you are seeing. And remember to be careful around this charged-up form of electricity.

Shocking, But True

A lightning bolt is a powerful display of electrical energy, but capturing that energy is difficult. It's almost impossible to predict exactly where lightning will strike. And when it does strike, it can be very destructive. Any equipment designed to receive lightning strikes would need to be completely unbreakable!

There are other problems, too. The actual electrical blast of a lightning strike is so quick that the energy is nearly impossible to store. And although lightning is electrical, much of that electrical energy changes into other forms of energy. Some is changed into light energy. That is the flash of light that you see. Some is changed into heat energy. That heat energy is changed into sound energy, which is what you hear as thunder. Once the energy has changed forms, it is even harder to capture.

Electrical Power

Instead of lightning, we use other parts of nature to power our lives. Water, wind, sunlight, fuels, and other natural energy sources are all used to produce electricity.

For now, nearly all the electricity you use can be traced back to a power plant. At the power plant, a **generator** uses movement, or **mechanical energy**, to produce an electric current, or electrical energy. A natural energy source is put to work to produce the movement that the generator uses.

A generator moves a copper wire, or other conductor, through the north pole and south pole of a magnet. This movement produces an electric current that flows through the conductor.

How a Generator Works

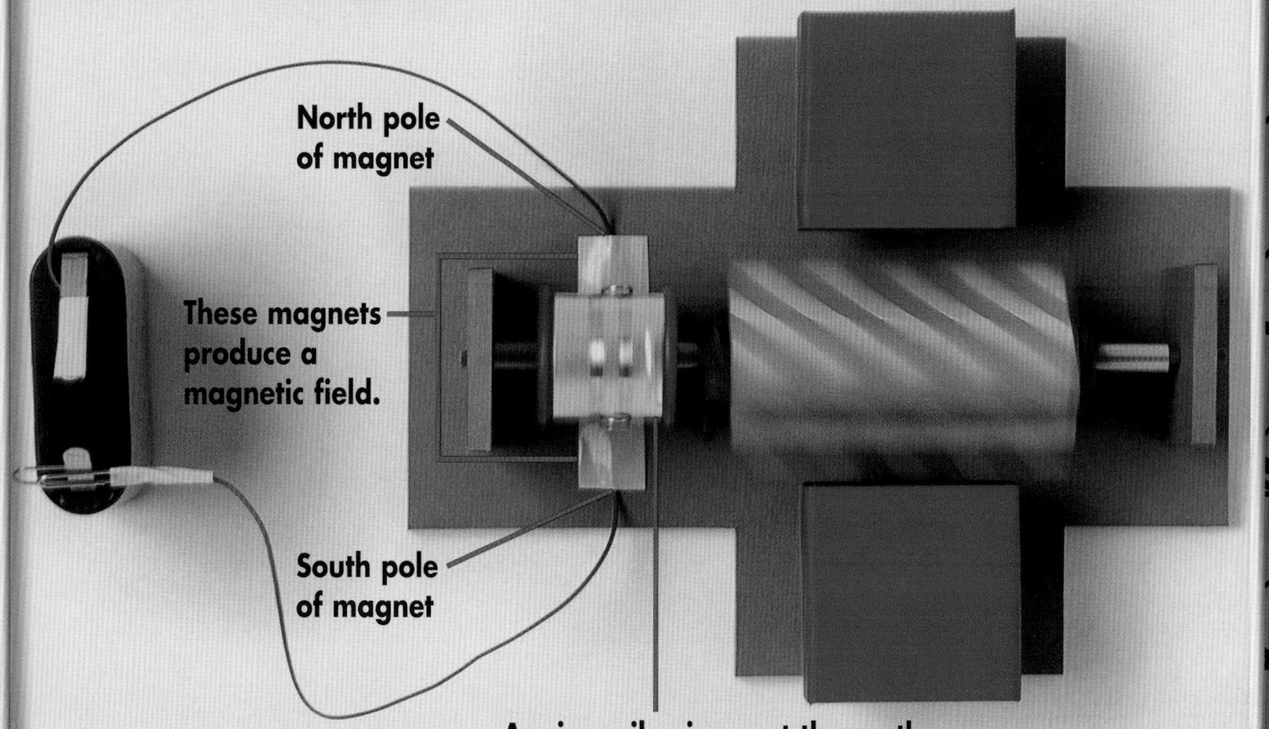

Wordwise

conductor: a material through which electricity can easily flow

electricity: a form of energy that involves the movement of electrons

generator: a device that changes mechanical energy into electrical energy

mechanical energy: the energy of motion

People Power

Did you know that electricity can also be people powered? Humans can provide the mechanical energy to power small generators. People-powered electricity can be used during a power outage or when a person is far away from an electrical outlet. And with people power, you never have to worry about extra batteries!

Light the Night. These bicycle lights have no batteries. As the bicyclists pedal, the generators produce electricity to power the lights.

When you have people-powered electricity, you can listen to the radio and make phone calls even when you're far away from electrical outlets. You could even use a computer!

You can use a mobile phone even if you don't have access to electricity. Just wind up this mobile phone and you're ready to call.

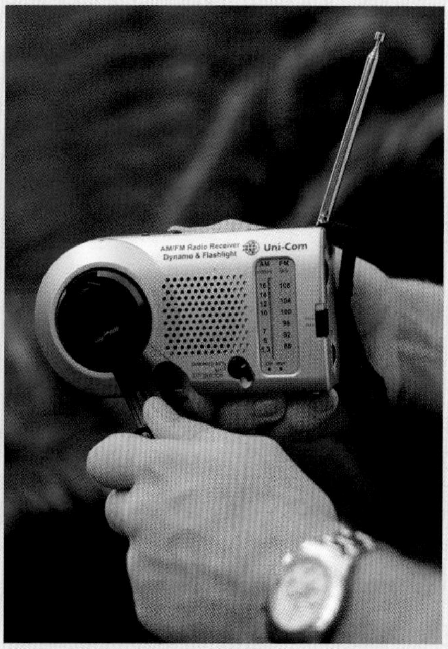

This radio is powered by a hand crank. Spinning the crank gets the generator going.

You probably flip a switch or push a button to turn on a light. These lights turn on with a pedal, shake, crank, or squeeze.

Power outage? No problem. The motion of shaking or squeezing gets this flashlight working.

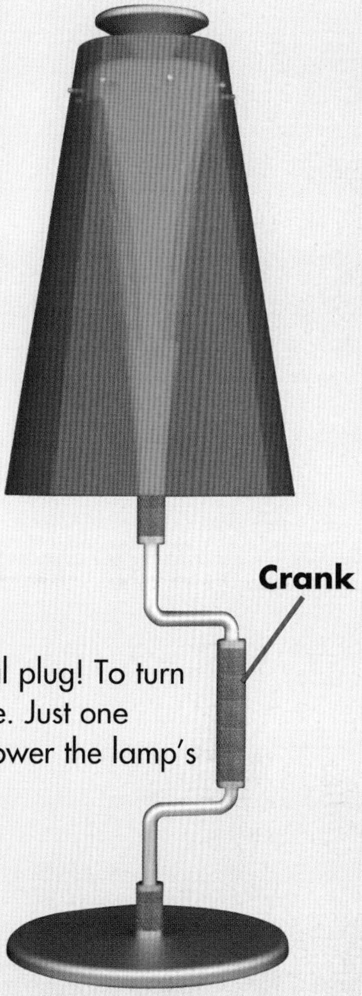

This lamp has no electrical plug! To turn it on you crank the handle. Just one minute of cranking can power the lamp's lightbulb for 40 minutes.

Lightning

Answer these shocking questions to find out what you learned.

1. What causes lightning?
2. Why isn't lightning used for electricity?
3. Why is lightning dangerous?
4. How does a generator work?
5. How can people power produce electricity?